SANJUAN

IN PRAISE OF

Sailing

IN PRAISE OF
Sailing

WELLERAN POLTARNEES

LAUGHING ELEPHANT

ISBN 1-883211-89-1

LAUGHING ELEPHANT BOOKS

3645 INTERLAKE AVENUE NORTH SEATTLE WASHINGTON 98103

WWW.LAUGHINGELEPHANT.COM

The rightness and beauty of a boat,

venturing forth on great waters

with only the winds and tides to carry it,

is one of life's supreme pleasures.

Our delight in this comes from deep within.

2

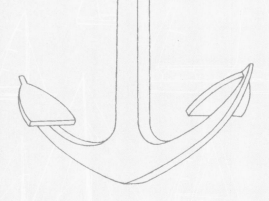

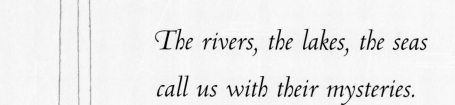

The rivers, the lakes, the seas
call us with their mysteries.

To sail is to escape to a place apart from our daily world.

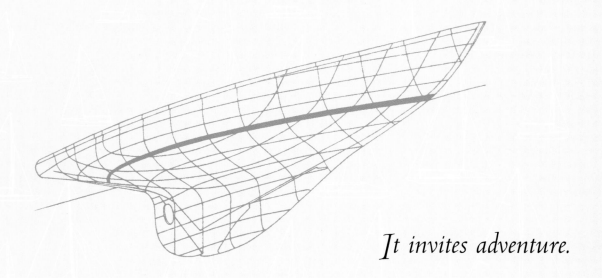

It invites adventure.

We have learned that the sea is a living being,

and that the mastery of a boat involves cooperation,

and the skillful application
of our inheritance of sailing lore.

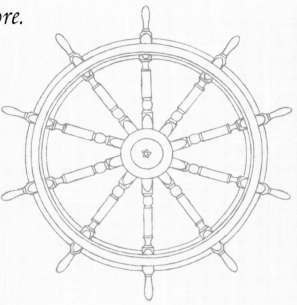

8

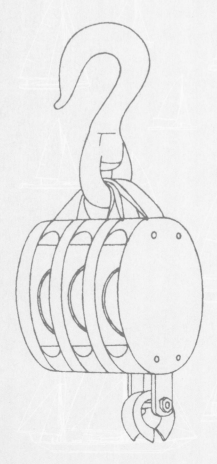

The vessels are wonderful to behold

whether they be slight or majestic,

old or new.

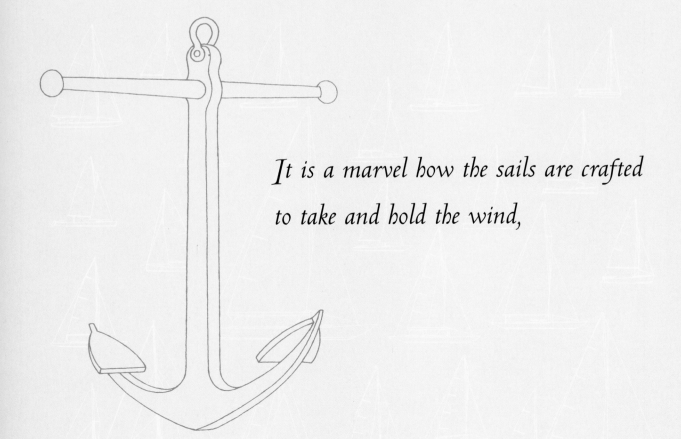

It is a marvel how the sails are crafted to take and hold the wind,

and the hulls to cleave the waters.

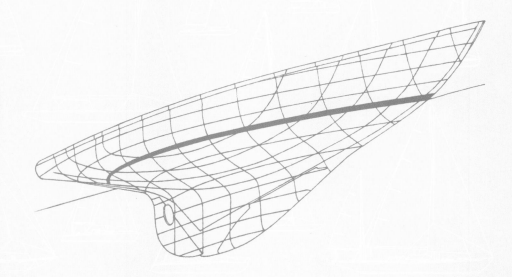

18

Gentle days on the water fill us with peace,

and heavy seas test our abilities and our courage.

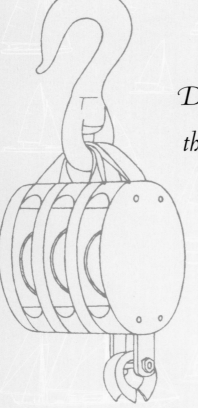

Days on the water offer delights to the body,

the mind, the spirit.

and we who sail enjoy, in our boats,

the sweetest kind of freedom.

PICTURE CREDITS

DESIGNED AT BLUE LANTERN STUDIO BY SACHEVERELL DARLING

TYPESET IN CENTAUR & CENTAUR SWASH CAPITALS